Friends

by Meg Greve

Content Consultants:
Melissa Z. Pierce, L.C.S.W.
Sam Williams, M.Ed.

Rourke
Educational Media
rourkeeducationalmedia.com

www.rourkeeducationalmedia.com

Melissa Z. Pierce is a licensed clinical social worker with a background in counseling in the home and school group settings. Melissa is currently a life coach. She brings her experience as a L.C.S.W. and parent to the *Little World Social Skills* collection and the *Social Skills and More* program.

Sam Williams has a master's degree in education. Sam Williams is a former teacher with over 10 years of classroom experience. He has been a literacy coach, professional development writer and trainer, and is a published author. He brings his experience in child development and classroom management to this series.

PHOTO CREDITS: Cover: © Rosemarie Gearhart; page 3: © kali9; page 5: © Agnieszka Kirinicjanow; page 7: © Chris Bernard; page 9: © kali9; page 11: © Chris Bernard; page 13: © Cliff Parnell; page 15: © Aldo Murillo; page 17: © Jennifer Conner; page 19: © digitalskillet; page 21: © Steve Debenport

Illustrations by: Anita DuFalla

Edited by: Precious McKenzie

Cover and Interior designed by: Tara Raymo

Library of Congress EPCN Data

Friends / Meg Greve
(Little World Social Skills)
ISBN 978-1-61810-129 7 (hard cover)(alk. paper)
ISBN 978-1-61810-262-1 (soft cover)
Library of Congress Control Number: 2011945273

Also Available as:

Rourke Educational Media
Printed in the United States of America,
North Mankato, Minnesota

rourkeeducationalmedia.com

customerservice@rourkeeducationalmedia.com • PO Box 643328 Vero Beach, Florida 32964

What is a friend?

A friend is someone you can **trust**. Friends help each other. Friends **share**.

Friends talk to each other and like being together. Friends treat each other **fairly**.

What do you and your friends like to do?

How do you make a friend?

Be friendly and helpful. Use nice words and listen to others.

Friends don't call each other names.

Treat others how you want to be treated.

Treat people with **respect**.
Give everyone a chance.

Sometimes friends **argue.**

Friends say they are **sorry**. Then they stay friends. A friend likes you for who you are, no matter what!

Take the Friendship Test!

1. I always try to treat my friends fairly. ◯ yes ◯ no

2. I share with my friends. ◯ yes ◯ no

3. My friends can trust me. ◯ yes ◯ no

4. I am a friend to others. ◯ yes ◯ no

5. I respect the feelings of others. ◯ yes ◯ no

Picture Glossary

argue (AHR-gyoo):
To fight with words.

fairly (FAIR-lee):
Acting trustworthy and reasonably.

respect (ri-SPEKT):
A feeling of thoughtfulness and recognition that something is important.

share (SHAIR):
To divide equally and take turns.

sorry (SAHR-ee):
Feeling sad or bad about doing something wrong.

trust (TRUHST):
Believing that someone is honest and will do what is promised.

Index

Websites

www.kidsgen.com/events/friendshipday/facts.htm

www.singdancelearn.com/character-education-songs/
friend-song/

www.scholastic.com/cliffordbebig/kids/
kids-slide-09.htm

About the Author

Meg Greve lives with her husband, daughter, and son. Her family has lots of friends and loves to be with them!

Meet The Author!
www.meetREMauthors.com